Includes Mobile Video Chapter Summaries

DESIRED FUTURE STATE

Growth Acceleration
Through Organizational
Alignment

JOHN MCNULTY

FREILING
AGENCY

Published by Freiling Agency, LLC.

P.O. Box 1264
Warrenton, VA 20188

www.FreilingAgency.com

PB ISBN: 978-1-963701-87-6
E-book ISBN: 978-1-963701-26-5

CONTENTS

INTRODUCTION

—〰—

My name is John McNulty. I'm the author and creator of *Desired Future State*®.

I've had a long career. Like most business people, I got my start doing grunt work in an entry-level position. From day one, I took myself and my job seriously. Through hard work, and with the help of many mentors along the way, I rose to the highest levels of some of America's most notable brands and organizations.

What I learned along the way is invaluable. It's now the goal of my life to impart this knowledge and these tools to you.

Needless to say, this book has been decades in the making. It presents a disciplined and proven method for kick-starting and managing growth acceleration at your organization.

What is "growth acceleration"? It's what the world's best executives think about every single day.

The fact is that simply increasing the bottom line year after year isn't enough to keep most businesses competitive. Seasoned and experienced business managers know this. The best organizations don't just grow, but they *accelerate* their growth. Through an aggressive and ever-evolving process of experimentation, trial and error, and strategic risk-taking, the executives who make the biggest difference and increase their company's market share find a way to make their companies *grow faster*.

This doesn't just mean beating last year's figures. It doesn't even mean growing at 25 percent, or even 50 percent, every single year.

Acceleration means to *speed up*. To break through ceilings and dominate your industry, you need to find ways to grow *exponentially faster*.

If you've picked up this book, I'm going to assume you're a business leader. Maybe you're a CEO or a CMO. Perhaps you're a VP or a senior director leading a large team. Maybe you're a founder and your team is too small for titles like these.

Regardless of title, this book is for leaders. It's for anyone who is pursuing a goal and leading a team. These lessons are for both life and business, but my particular method becomes especially valuable at the highest rungs of an organization.

The method is called Desired Future State. It's not just theoretical. I've used this logic throughout my career. It's led me straight to the top of some of the world's most successful brands. Sure, it can be nuanced, and it can be complicated. Putting these principles into practice requires discipline and focus every single day. But I guarantee that if you take this seriously, you'll find success. Desired Future State has been the cornerstone of my professional career, spanning several decades. And as long as I'm alive, that's never going to change.

My professional journey started at Indiana University of Pennsylvania. I majored in behavioral science and took my studies seriously. After I graduated, I was recruited by a prestigious social service agency in Harrisburg, Pennsylvania. This agency specialized in providing change-management counseling to troubled youth and families. My manager, Liz—a brilliant PhD—played a pivotal role in my early professional development. Liz was highly skilled in deploying a change-management methodology that, while informal and untitled, was remarkably effective.

We worked hard. The weeks were long. But every Friday afternoon, Liz and I would meet to review my caseloads. These reviews focused on how we could most effectively accelerate our clients from their troubled present state (current state) to the more stable and successful future they desired (desired future state). We discussed challenges and obstacles. We launched initiatives to overcome them. We carefully defined metrics, set goals, and determined timelines. Although we never formalized this process with a name, it was a highly effective change-management methodology. It helped troubled people to start making the changes they wanted to make and to start doing it faster.

I didn't know it at the time, but my experience with Liz—her mentorship, ideas, and commitment to investing in me—became the foundational pillar of all my professional success.

After nearly four years working with Liz in Harrisburg, I was recruited by the Gillette Company. They wanted me to join their sales organization, working out of the Philadelphia District Office. Things took off. Over the next ten years, I was promoted eight times. I moved steadily and readily through various levels of sales and marketing leadership at Gillette, and I attribute much of this success to the principles Liz instilled into me. I also credit Ron, my personal mentor while I worked at Gillette. His unrelenting focus on accelerating the growth of individuals and teams—helping them move from their *current state* to their *desired future state*—was extraordinary.

Ron and I worked tirelessly. We developed systems to formalize what had brought our teams so much success, incorporating much of what I had learned from Liz. We stuck to these systems religiously, and we experienced profound success that we could clearly and unambiguously attribute to the logic we put in place.

After about ten years at Gillette, I was recruited by Alberto Culver—now a division of Unilever. At Alberto Culver, I once again had the good fortune to report to a skilled and experienced mentor, JohnnyB, who quickly became one of the most important people in my career's evolution. He dedicated a significant amount of his time and energy to helping me. His input and advice accelerated the success I began having at Alberto Culver, and people started to notice.

Unbeknownst to me, I was building a reputation in the corporate world as a growth acceleration guru. The logic I'd carefully designed over the previous twenty years—with the help of Liz, Ron, and JohnnyB—was in demand, and I began to formalize these systems into something I could readily share and apply across the spectrum of corporate verticals, departments, and other circumstances.

I called it Desired Future State, and it's been the bedrock of my corporate work ever since. It's how I think about everything from setting sales and operations goals to recruiting and developing talent to reviewing performance and holding team members accountable. Desired Future State is now copyright protected. This is my A-to-Z plan for accelerating an organization's growth, and it always works because it forces organizational alignment around the lifeblood of any company. And that is profitable revenue growth acceleration.

Eventually, with my Desired Future State methodology in hand, I was offered and accepted leadership positions at several growth-challenged organizations. I was vice president at Wilson Sporting Goods; vice president and general manager at Eastman Kodak; senior vice president at Brunswick Corporation; president of MacGregor Golf Company; and CEO and co-founder of Didgebridge, a Web3.0 marketing technology company.

Needless to say, I've been busy. But when I reflect on my career, I've really been doing the same thing all along—just under different brands and alongside different people. My career has been defined by successfully accelerating growth at organizations with people who were willing to do what it takes to get it done.

And what does it take? That's what this book is about.

I wrote this book to help you accelerate growth in your team or at your organization, no matter how big or how small. By adopting and adapting this methodology, you will overcome the obstacles that have, maybe for many years, stood between you and multiplying your organization's growth. I'll share high-level models for how to think about accelerating growth. I'll share real-world scripts and examples for getting this done. I'll dive into common pitfalls and challenges leaders face in implementing these principles and the best practices for overcoming them. I want you to be 100 percent equipped to put these principles into practice.

Because the fact is this: It's impossible for me to exaggerate the value of this system. It's worked for me and dozens of my colleagues, coworkers, and counterparts. And I guarantee it will work for you. I'll always be grateful to those mentors and coworkers who helped me define and refine it over the years. I know, without a doubt, that Desired Future State can and will bring incredible success to your organization.

1

INTRODUCTION TO THE TRANSFORMATION JOURNEY

Interactive Video Chapter Summary

Or text **journey** to 855-426-7770

By scanning this QR code and sending the keyword you are consenting to join the author's SMS loyalty program. We do not share your data with third parties. Msg&Data Rates May Apply. Msg Freq Varies. Send HELP for help, reply STOP to 855.426.7770 to end.

Imagine setting sail on a ship bound for an in-name-only destination. Picture the vast, open sea stretching out before you with no clear path to follow and no landmarks to guide you.

What does that mean? Well, it means you know where you want to go, but you don't know how to get there. You have an end goal in mind, a vision of your desired destination, but the steps to reach it are uncertain, filled with unpredictability and challenges.

That's what it should feel like to be on the journey of growth. This is not a straightforward path but a winding road with twists and turns. It involves navigating through unknown waters, learning from each experience, and continually adjusting your course. The journey of growth is about embracing the uncertainty, finding strength in the face of obstacles, and persisting despite setbacks.

Growth is about becoming something that you're not. If you knew what it looked and felt like to grow, and exactly how to get there, you'd be there already—no need for a "journey." But growth isn't like that. Growing—both as a person and as an organization—involves perilous waters, lots of uncertainty, and endless trial and error along the way. It is a continual process that requires constant effort, adaptation, and resilience in the face of challenges.

Growth isn't a sudden transformation. Nor is it something you can simply set into motion once and reap the benefits later. It demands sustained commitment and the willingness to learn and evolve over time.

The kind of growth that truly pushes things forward is an ongoing, fluid process; it's a metamorphosis from your current state—your present, on-the-ground reality—to a desired future state that you can't always picture ahead of time. This transformation is gradual and often unpredictable, necessitating a deep understanding of your goals and the flexibility to adjust your strategies as you progress. It's about envisioning a future that may be unclear and working tirelessly to bring that vision to life, despite the obstacles that might arise.

At its essence, the growth journey is about breaking free from inertia. It's about mustering the courage to scrutinize yourself and your organization, warts and all, and recognizing the vast chasm that separates your current reality from your future aspirations. This chasm can be big or small, and it can seem insurmountable at times, yet it is always there, challenging you to bridge it.

The growth journey is not for the fainthearted. It demands a vision as clear as crystal even without the help of a detailed map—a vision that can be your guiding star as you navigate choppy waters and turbulent seas. It calls for an unflinchingly honest assessment of your organization's current state, delving into every nook and cranny, uncovering hidden flaws and unspoken truths. It requires strategic planning that transcends quarterly reports, looking decades ahead despite the darkness that clouds your vision, and envisioning a future that is vibrant and full of potential. And it requires an unyielding resolve to surmount the inevitable obstacles that will test your limits and demand your utmost perseverance.

But here's the thing: If I'm successful with this book, by the time you turn the last page, you'll hold in your hands a definite, powerful, and game-changing roadmap to achieving the growth your organization so desperately needs. My goal is to provide the tools, insights, and strategies that will empower you to break through barriers, seize opportunities, and realize your full potential. With each chapter, you will gain a deeper understanding of the dynamics of growth, the principles that underpin it, and the practical steps you can take to make it a reality.

But this book is more than a mere guide. It's an invitation to take that leap of faith, to step boldly into the unknown, and to emerge transformed, prepared to seize the future that awaits you with open arms. It encourages you to embrace the uncertainties and challenges that lie ahead with courage and resilience.

This isn't about change for change's sake. It's not about hopping on the latest bandwagon of trends and buzzwords that may fade away tomorrow. This journey is about intentional, meaningful change and careful, sustainable growth that stands the test of time. It's about shedding old skins, breaking free from outdated mindsets and systems that no longer serve you, and adopting a new, vibrant form—one that's agile and adaptable enough to navigate the challenges and opportunities of the ever-evolving business landscape.

Transformation is about transcending your status quo, pushing boundaries, and daring to envision a future radically different from the present. It's about recognizing the disparities between where your organization currently is and where it aspires to be. This journey demands a clear, compelling vision for the future; a thorough examination of your current state; and strategic planning grounded in reality yet driven by ambition. It requires the steadfast determination to overcome the hurdles that lie between you and the future you want and the perseverance to see it through.

This book is your mentor and partner, guiding you to identify the gaps, develop a strategic action plan, and implement changes that will lead to a profound transformation. It empowers you to take control of your destiny and create a sustainable, thriving future for your organization.

IMPORTANCE OF MOVING FROM CURRENT STATE TO DESIRED FUTURE STATE

In the ever-shifting landscape of today's business environment, the role of growth transformation is paramount for the success and longevity of any organization. It's not merely an option but a fundamental necessity for any organization aiming to survive and flourish in a competitive market. Great leaders understand this intrinsic need for transformation and the continual evolution of their business strategies. They recognize that complacency and maintaining the status quo are not just ineffective strategies but are pathways to obsolescence and eventual failure. These leaders are proactive, constantly seeking innovative ways to enhance their operations, adapt to changing market demands, and anticipate future trends. By fostering a culture of growth and encouraging their teams to embrace change, they ensure that their organizations remain resilient, agile, and poised for long-term success.

To truly compete, organizations must commit to accelerating growth, fostering relentless innovation, and swiftly adapting to the ever-changing market dynamics. This journey from your organization's current state to its desired future state is not merely about survival; it's about thriving and dominating the field. Survival and thriving, in this context, become indistinguishable. This journey harnesses the untapped potential within your organization, refines it, and aligns it with an ambitious yet attainable vision for the future. It's about sculpting a future that transcends current limitations and carves out a competitive edge in the marketplace.

Over the years, I've distilled my diverse and varied experiences into a comprehensive methodology that I call Desired Future State. This battle-tested approach provides a disciplined, rigorous framework that is essential for initiating, managing, and sustaining significant growth acceleration within any organization. It's a detailed blueprint for organizational transformation that I have meticulously honed through years of executive leadership roles and practical, hands-on application in various business scenarios. This toolkit is as profound in its conceptual depth as it is practical in its application, making it a versatile resource for leaders.

At the very core of the Desired Future State approach lies the fundamental principle of leveraging an organization's existing capabilities to their fullest potential. It places immense value on the latent assets and resources that are already present within the organization but are often underused. These assets are waiting to be harnessed and directed toward a clear, forward-thinking vision. This vision acts as a guiding beacon, illuminating the path and steering the organization toward exponential growth and unparalleled success. By effectively using the Desired Future State methodology, organizations can achieve a transformative journey that not only meets but also exceeds their growth aspirations.

The journey to the desired future state isn't just about reaching a final destination. It's also about the myriad benefits that come along the way. These benefits are both significant and varied. They include enhanced operational efficiency, enabling an organization to deliver products or services more effectively and at a lower cost. Improved customer satisfaction is another benefit, fostering stronger relationships, greater loyalty, and a robust market reputation.

Moreover, this journey often results in increased market share, a testament to an organization's competitive prowess. Crucially, it also leads to a more motivated and aligned workforce. When employees understand and commit to the shared vision laid out by their leaders, their engagement and productivity soar. I've observed this phenomenon countless times.

The Desired Future State approach is about converting potential into performance, vision into reality, and aspirations into tangible achievements. It's about rethinking growth and accelerating the journey toward a more prosperous, sustainable, and successful future.

KEY THEMES IN TRANSFORMATION

At a bird's-eye level, this book revolves around several pivotal themes. Each one of these will be integral to your organization's transformation journey:

1. **Assessment:** The first step is to grasp the current state of your organization. This isn't a cursory glance; it's a deep dive into your team's existing processes, capabilities, and challenges.

This assessment needs to be precise and unbiased, setting the stage for the planning and decisions that will steer you toward your desired future state.

2. **Vision Creation:** Crafting a clear and compelling vision for the future is essential. This vision acts as both your map and your guiding light. It's the destination that keeps your team members aligned and motivated, guiding them toward your desired future state.

3. **Strategic Planning:** Bridging the gap between the current state and the desired future state requires creating a detailed roadmap. This involves setting SMART goals (more on this later), pinpointing key initiatives, and ensuring cross-departmental collaboration. This is an ongoing journey that never truly ends.

4. **Implementation and Change Management:** Putting your transformation plan into action demands meticulous planning and effective change management techniques. This includes communicating your vision, engaging stakeholders, and maintaining

your team's momentum throughout the implementation process.

5. **Measurement and Continual Improvement:** Tracking success through metrics and key performance indicators (KPIs) is vital for monitoring your organization's progress. Regular reviews of team members and goals, coupled with appropriate adjustments based on those reviews, provide the essential course corrections that will make or break your desired future state journey.

Each of these steps holds equal importance. They must be tackled in sequence—you can't chart a course until you know your starting point. And you can't correct your path until you've embarked on one.

Keep these five steps in mind as you read on.

BENEFITS OF ACHIEVING A DESIRED FUTURE STATE

Transformation is the comprehensive and profound process of fundamentally changing the way an organization operates, encompassing its culture, systems, structures, and processes to achieve significant and sustained improvements in performance, outcomes, and overall effectiveness. It involves rethinking and redesigning the very fabric of an organization to adapt to evolving market demands, technological advancements, and competitive pressures.

My professional journey, as detailed in the introduction, provides a rich tapestry of experiences and insights that underscore the critical role of transformation in achieving growth acceleration. This journey highlights the numerous challenges and opportunities encountered along the way and how the application of strategic transformation initiatives can lead to substantial organizational growth. My Desired Future State methodology delves into a systematic and structured approach to change, offering a roadmap for organizations to navigate the complexities of transformation effectively. This methodology illustrates how organizations can not only survive but thrive by embracing change, fostering innovation, and continually seeking ways to enhance their performance and success.

By deeply understanding and consistently applying the core principles of transformation, leaders can position their organizations for enduring and sustainable success. This involves not just implementing change, but also cultivating a mindset of continual improvement, resilience, and adaptability. Through this approach, organizations can build a strong foundation for long-term growth, ensuring they remain competitive and relevant in an ever-changing business landscape.

Achieving a desired future state offers numerous benefits for an organization:

- **Enhanced Organizational Alignment:** When everyone in an organization understands and is committed to one shared vision, it fosters a culture of unity and shared purpose.

- **Improved Efficiency and Effectiveness:** Streamlined processes and clear goals lead to better use of resources and higher productivity.

- **Increased Market Competitiveness:** Organizations that successfully transform can better respond to market trends and customer needs, gaining a competitive edge.

- **Employee Engagement and Satisfaction:** A clear and inspiring vision motivates employees, leading to higher engagement and job satisfaction.

- **Sustainable Growth:** By aligning strategies and operations with long-term goals, organizations can achieve sustainable growth and profitability.

The subsequent chapters will dive deeper into the processes and strategies necessary to achieve this transformation, providing practical insights and real-world examples to guide you along the way.

2

ASSESSING THE CURRENT STATE

Interactive Video Chapter Summary

Or text **current state** to 855-426-7770

By scanning this QR code and sending the keyword you are consenting to join the author's SMS loyalty program. We do not share your data with third parties. Msg&Data Rates May Apply. Msg Freq Varies. Send HELP for help, reply STOP to 855.426.7770 to end.

"The journey of a thousand miles begins with one step."

That's an old saying—thousands of years old, in fact. And it's as true now as it's ever been.

Every journey begins with one step. And if my experience is worth anything, the people and organizations that make it to their destinations usually take that first step in the right direction.

But here's the funny thing about achieving your desired future state: Your first step is actually to take one big step backward.

Why?

Because you can't know where you're going until you know where you are. Maps are useless if there's no "YOU ARE HERE" marker.

In the Desired Future State model, this is called assessing your Current State. I capitalized those words for a reason. Current State is very specific, and it is the foundation of everything we'll do going forward. The better you understand your organization's Current State, the more efficient your team will be as they plow ahead toward your Desired Future State.

Without a clear beginning, you'll never make it to your destination. Everything starts with assessing your Current State.

METHODS FOR ASSESSING THE CURRENT STATE

Over the years, I've had the opportunity to help numerous organizations assess their Current State. This process often involved deep dives into an organization's operations, culture, and overall performance metrics to get a clear picture of where it stood.

I was often the person leading these organizations and efforts, entrusted with the significant responsibility of setting the stage and casting a compelling vision to engage hundreds, or even thousands, of employees. This included not only strategic planning but also the hands-on work of motivating and aligning large teams toward common goals.

Other times, I played the role of an advisor, providing critical insights and recommendations from an external standpoint, or I contributed on the ground level as a dedicated team member, working alongside others to implement changes and improvements.

Across my decades of experience, I can say confidently that assessing your Current State can take many forms, each tailored to the unique needs and circumstances of the organization. Some organizations find great success with **SWOT analyses.** These are powerful and structured analytical tools that help you identify your organization's **S**trengths, **W**eaknesses, **O**pportunities, and **T**hreats. When executed effectively, a SWOT analysis provides a balanced and multi-angle view of your organization's internal capabilities and external challenges. This thorough examination depends on including key team members and stakeholders from various departments, ensuring diverse perspectives. It may even be beneficial to incorporate a third-party perspective from outside your organization to ensure a comprehensive and unbiased analysis. By doing so, the SWOT analysis not only highlights areas for improvement but also uncovers potential opportunities for growth and innovation.

Other organizations dive deeply into their employees' and stakeholders' minds through intense (and sometimes grueling) listening sessions, which can last for hours and cover a wide range of topics. This kind of **stakeholder feedback** can be truly game-changing and transformative for your organization. Your employees, after all, are on the front lines, dealing every single day with the operations of your organization, encountering both routine and unexpected challenges. They have invaluable insights that no executives can possibly have, and they often possess innovative ideas on how to make things work better due to their unique perspectives and daily experiences.

This kind of feedback can be gathered through various methods such as one-on-one interviews, online surveys, or focus groups. One-on-one interviews can provide deep, personal insights, while online surveys can capture a broader range of opinions quickly. Focus groups, on the other hand, enable interactive discussions that can spark new ideas and solutions. Regardless of the method, the goal is to collect comprehensive and diverse insights from a host of perspectives other than your own. Ideally, the way you conduct this kind of research will be custom tailored to account for the nuances of your unique organization, including its culture, size, and industry-specific challenges.

Then, of course, using **performance metrics** can offer a quantitative and data-informed picture of your organization's current state along any number of dynamics. These metrics, when created and updated accurately, can include a wide range of data points such as sales figures, customer satisfaction scores, and operational efficiency indicators. By providing concrete data, these metrics can greatly enhance your Current State assessment with invaluable insights and details.

Moreover, this might even extend to benchmarking your organization's performance against that of your competitors. Depending on your industry, access to this comparative data might be relatively easy to obtain, which can offer an additional layer of context and understanding.

It's crucial to analyze these metrics over time to identify trends and patterns that may influence your transformation efforts. Regularly reviewing these data points allows you to spot emerging trends, understand cyclical patterns, and anticipate potential challenges or opportunities. This ongoing analysis ensures that your strategic decisions are well-informed and grounded in solid evidence, thereby increasing the chances of successful transformation.

These are just some ideas. The bottom line is to be sure that any assessment of your Current State is thorough and as unbiased as possible.

IMPORTANCE OF AN OBJECTIVE ASSESSMENT

No matter how you conduct your Current State assessment, maintaining objectivity is critical. I've seen it happen many times before—biases and preconceived notions creep into Current State assessments and cloud executives' thinking and judgment. These biases can stem from personal experiences, past successes, or even failures, which might lead to an inaccurate portrayal of the current situation.

That's why, when it comes to assessing your Current State, honesty is the best policy. This isn't a time for rose-colored glasses. The best Current State assessments I've been part of were uncomfortable—nothing held back, nothing left unsaid. The process might involve having difficult conversations, confronting harsh realities, and facing the facts head-on. While this might not be fun, the more accurate you are about how things *really* look on the ground, the faster will be your progress toward your Desired Future State. This accuracy sets a solid foundation for any future strategies and plans, ensuring they are rooted in reality.

In other words, assessing your Current State isn't about anyone's opinion. It's about the cold, hard facts. Is high employee morale part of your Current State? Then prove it with data, such as employee satisfaction surveys or retention rates. Is poor sales performance part of your Current State? Then that should be clear and obvious in your sales figures, customer feedback, and market analysis. Bring justification for your Current State conclusions, and don't be afraid to speak up. Use quantifiable data and concrete evidence to support your assessments, ensuring that your evaluation is based on solid ground rather than assumptions or wishful thinking.

One particularly effective way to ensure objectivity during your Current State assessment is to engage external experts who can provide a mostly unbiased view of your organization. These experts can conduct their own independent assessments and offer fresh insights. They often identify blind spots that you and your department heads may overlook, which can be crucial for a comprehensive evaluation.

No, this doesn't have to mean bringing in expensive McKinsey consultants. If you're a CEO or VP, chances are you know someone at another organization who might gladly participate in your Current State assessment—someone who's not tied up in your day-to-day activities and who might be able to offer a more unbiased perspective. This is an opportunity for that person as much as it is for you. Don't hesitate to ask trusted colleagues who you believe will be honest. They might even appreciate the chance to see how another organization operates and gain insights themselves.

But you don't necessarily need a third party. The bottom line is simply to gain an accurate understanding of your Current State and what's working in your organization and what needs to change to start moving toward your Desired Future State. The data for this assessment exists inside your organization—you just need to be willing to find and analyze it. This can involve detailed internal surveys, comprehensive data analysis, and even employee interviews to gather as much information as possible. By taking the time to properly assess your Current State, you set a strong foundation for the strategic decisions that will drive your organization forward.

CASE STUDIES OF SUCCESSFUL ASSESSMENTS

Time and again, I've witnessed firsthand the impact of successful assessments on an organization's growth transformation.

Arriving at a successful assessment can be challenging, especially when it comes to aligning an organization around the company's true Current State. This process often requires consultative, neutral guidance from an external strategic consulting firm. In my career, we frequently invited key customers to participate and provide a Current State assessment from their perspective. This customer assessment is vitally important, as an organization's growth acceleration may largely depend on it.

Here's an example of this challenge from my tenure as senior vice president at Brunswick. I was recruited to Brunswick to help turn around (accelerate growth), as part of a leadership team, two struggling acquisitions the company had recently made. Right off the bat, there was significant friction and internal disagreement regarding the Current State assessment. Sales had strong opinions, as did marketing, operations, customer service, and finance. We were struggling to arrive at any kind of Current State alignment. Without this alignment, it would be nearly impossible for the functional heads to agree upon the Desired Future State, to accurately identify the obstacles preventing progress toward our Desired Future State, or to launch the right initiatives to overcome these obstacles.

To overcome this lack of Current State consensus, we sought input from key customers. We arranged a meeting with our largest customer, which took place at a major trade show. Our attendees at the meeting included our Brunswick division's functional heads for sales, marketing, finance, customer service, and manufacturing/operations.

To our surprise, our customer used a form of dark humor to describe his assessment of our Current State. He put it bluntly: "Your company makes overpriced junk, and you ship it late."

This was uncomfortable to hear. I remember the steely faces in the room—how are we supposed to respond to that? But this was a feedback session, not a sales meeting. No response was needed.

When our multifunctional team later convened, we admitted that this customer had, indeed, provided an accurate assessment. This was, after all, our largest customer; it didn't matter whether we thought he was right or wrong. It became apparent to all of us that every functional area had some changes to make if we were to accelerate growth to our Desired Future State. The customer's words echoed in our minds:

"Overpriced junk and shipped late."

This led us to ask critical questions: Are our prices too high? Do we need to reduce them? Is our quality control lacking, resulting in our products being perceived as junk? Do we need to change our supply chains? And finally, why are our deliveries late? Is there an issue with our on-time deliveries and customer satisfaction?

As we pondered these questions, we realized the importance of aligning our organization's perspective with that of our customers. The path to growth acceleration was clear: we needed to address this problem, and quickly. This is what it would mean for us to achieve growth and progress toward our Desired Future State where our products were not overpriced and were not junk!

THE ROLE OF LEADERS IN THE ASSESSMENT PROCESS

Leaders play a crucial role in the Current State assessment process, and their involvement is pivotal to its success.

As a leader, your responsibility is to set the tone for the assessment, ensuring that it is approached with openness and objectivity. You need to foster a culture of transparency where employees feel comfortable sharing their honest feedback and insights. It is important to create an environment where contradicting their claims or even slightly insinuating that their feedback is wrong or misguided is avoided at all costs. Such actions will disable your Current State assessment from the get-go.

Therefore, be open and willing to hear every perspective. When you don't agree, just note that privately—this isn't the time to get defensive. Embrace constructive criticism as a tool for growth and improvement.

Your role as a leader also involves guiding the assessment process, from defining the scope and objectives to selecting the appropriate tools and techniques. This means carefully planning each step and ensuring that all team members are aware of the process and its importance. By actively participating in the assessment, you demonstrate your commitment to understanding the current state and driving positive change. Make it clear that these meetings are not just routine but are essential for the organization's development. Nobody in the room should be unclear about what's going on and why these meetings are happening. All attendees should believe, even if they don't buy in yet, that these meetings can help bring about the kind of growth transformation *everyone* on your team should eagerly want. Additionally, illustrate how past assessments have led to significant improvements, thereby reinforcing the value of their involvement and feedback.

In summary, your leadership in the Current State assessment process is indispensable. By setting the right tone, fostering transparency, and guiding the process meticulously, you can ensure that the assessment yields valuable insights and paves the way for meaningful progress. Your commitment and active participation will inspire your team and drive the organization toward a brighter future.

PITFALLS TO AVOID

While assessing the Current State is essential, several very common pitfalls should be avoided. One of the most significant is the tendency to overlook or downplay weaknesses. It's natural to focus on strengths and successes, but understanding your organization's weaknesses is critical for effective transformation. For instance, when our customer bluntly told us our products were overpriced and "junk," it was an uncomfortable realization. However, these uncomfortable truths are crucial. The more uncomfortable you are during this assessment phase, the better the insights you will gain. The point is to identify these problems so they can be fixed—not to avoid the hard topics altogether. Recognizing and addressing these weaknesses head-on can pave the way for substantial improvements and long-term success.

Another pitfall is relying solely on internal perspectives. While internal assessments and feedback from your team members are valuable, as they are the ones who know what it's like to work at your organization day after day, their assessments can often be biased or limited in scope. Sometimes, internal team members worry about their job security and may hesitate to bring up problems or weaknesses. Additionally, they might have turned a blind eye to problems for so long that they now have significant blind spots, making it impossible for them to specifically identify problem areas. This is why incorporating external viewpoints can provide a more balanced and objective understanding of your organization's current state. As I mentioned earlier, this doesn't have to mean hiring an expensive third-party consultant (although that might be a good idea). At Brunswick, we asked our biggest customer for feedback. On other teams I've led, we've brought in a vendor or other partner—sometimes even an old friend—to provide an outsider's perspective on a Current State assessment. Most seasoned business professionals will be happy to participate in this kind of work, especially if it involves some form of compensation or recognition. I've never regretted pulling in an outsider's perspective, as it often highlights areas we might have overlooked internally.

Finally, avoid rushing through the assessment process. It can be tempting to get this done quickly so you can move on to making the kinds of changes that will bring about your growth transformation. But don't give in to this temptation! Thoroughness is key to a good Current State assessment. Taking the time to be thorough allows you to identify the root causes of issues and develop effective solutions. Take all the time you need to gather comprehensive data, analyze it carefully from a variety of perspectives, and ensure that your assessment provides a solid foundation for the next steps in your growth transformation journey. By being meticulous and deliberate, you can ensure that the steps you take next will be well-informed and strategic, leading to a more successful transformation.

CONCLUSION

Assessing your organization's Current State is the first and arguably the most crucial step in any transformation journey. It sets the stage for everything that follows, providing the insights and understanding needed to define your desired future state and develop a roadmap to get there. Think of it as how you line up your ladder—being just a few inches off at the beginning means ending up potentially far away from where you want to be at the top.

By approaching the assessment with care, objectivity, thoroughness, and a commitment to improvement, you will lay the groundwork for a successful transformation that will propel your organization toward its Desired Future State.

3

DEFINING THE DESIRED FUTURE STATE

Interactive Video Chapter Summary

Or text **future state** to 855-426-7770

Defining your organization's Desired Future State is the next step in any successful growth transformation process.

You never get to where you're going if you don't know where you're going.

This stage is about envisioning where you want your organization to be in the future and charting a course to get there. This chapter will help you to create a clear, compelling, and achievable Desired Future State vision that will guide your organization toward its goals. In my experience, this step is not about setting lofty aspirations, but it's about crafting a nuanced and organization-specific vision that aligns with your core values and is rooted deep in reality.

GATHERING DESIRED FUTURE STATE INFORMATION

The process of defining your Desired Future State begins with gathering insights from all corners of your organization and understanding the various perspectives that exist within it. This comprehensive approach ensures that no critical viewpoint is overlooked and every potential angle is considered.

I always start this process by asking each department head to summarize his or her vision for the future in just three bullet points. Yes, just bullet points, and just three of them. This might seem overly simplistic, but it is a powerful method that forces your team members to be clear and focused on their priorities. You don't want a laundry list of little things or a general repository of to-do items. Defining your Desired Future State is about distilling the many and complex moving parts in your organization and its culture into simple, actionable ideas—specific things that, if achieved, will fix problems and set the stage for a future of growth and success.

Each department head must work independently on this effort. Instruct your department heads not to consult with each other when crafting their bullet points. This ensures each summary reflects one's unique perspective, which might be tainted with someone else's ideas if it were to be run by a colleague. This also helps to prevent "groupthink," which I've seen hamper the efforts of many organizations to leverage the full brainpower of their teams. We want a diversity of insights that can come only from independent thought. By ensuring these summaries are created in isolation, you foster a wide array of innovative ideas that can drive your organization forward in unexpected and fruitful ways.

By gathering these focused, independently created summaries, you lay the groundwork for a clear, actionable strategy that integrates the diverse perspectives of your entire leadership team. This holistic approach not only clarifies the path ahead but also strengthens the unity and direction of your organization, aligning everyone toward a shared vision of the future.

Give your team members *one week* to come up with their bullet points. These don't have to be just one sentence, but they need to be concise—a paragraph at most. Why just one week? Because by setting a one-week deadline, you'll maintain the kind of momentum needed to make your organization's growth transformation happen and ensure that the ultimate vision remains relevant and forward-looking.

THE OFF-SITE VISION MEETING

Once the summaries are prepared, it's time to bring everyone together for a pivotal Reveal and Discuss meeting. This is one of my favorite parts of the Desired Future State program. Holding this meeting off-site is crucial. It creates a neutral environment where open dialogue and honest feedback can flourish, and it boosts feelings of camaraderie among your team members who might not often work with each other.

Picture your leadership team gathered in a relaxed setting, away from the daily grind. Each department head presents his or her vision, sharing the three bullet points. This isn't just a presentation. It's an opportunity for each leader to articulate aspirations and to rally support for one's vision. As each vision is revealed, engage your team in a robust question-and-answer discussion to identify common themes and potential misalignments between the bullet points brought forth by each department head. Disagreement is normal and even good. But accept, and don't reject, your team's bullet points and suggestions. Their final form may not be exactly what they first present, but if they did their due diligence in crafting their suggestions, any corrections would be about clarifying the real issues—not putting anyone's ideas down altogether.

Indeed, it's common to discover that different departments have varying priorities and perspectives on the future. For instance, your marketing team might be focused on brand expansion while your operations team could be more concerned with optimizing current shipping and manufacturing processes. These differing viewpoints can provide a more comprehensive understanding of the company's overall needs and goals.

Recognizing these differences is crucial for building a cohesive vision. Here's a case study from my career. In one of the companies where I worked, we faced a similar situation. Our sales department was pushing for aggressive market penetration strategies while the finance team was advocating for a cautious approach to manage risks and ensure financial stability.

By bringing these perspectives to the table, we were able to balance ambition with prudence, leading to a well-rounded strategy that satisfied both departments.

Ultimately, this meeting is not just about presenting ideas but about fostering a collaborative environment where every team member feels valued and heard. It's about building a unified vision that everyone is committed to achieving. When done correctly, the Reveal and Discuss meeting can be a transformative experience for your organization, setting the stage for future success.

During my tenure as vice president at Wilson Sporting Goods, I was part of a growth-acceleration turnaround team for the USA Golf Division. Despite the brand having one of the most powerful and iconic brand names in golf history, Wilson's golf division was struggling with growth acceleration.

Upon joining Wilson, I quickly realized—along with most of my turnaround team—that cohesive organizational alignment was lacking. Thus far, they had papered over some pretty significant areas of disagreement. In their particular case, much of this tension revolved around two specific strategic challenges:

1. Manufacturing in USA versus manufacturing in Asia

2. Distribution and sales channels in the USA

For Wilson, these internal (and sometimes heated) debates involved all of the organization's functional areas—finance, manufacturing, global sourcing, customer service, sales, and marketing. There was no shortage of strong, differing opinions at Wilson, and organizational alignment was simply not happening. Consequently, Wilson's prestigious, tradition-rich USA Golf Division was not successful.

It was my strong opinion that changes to their Desired Future State had to be made, and they had to be made fast.

To tackle this challenge, we instituted multi-functional teams by product groups—golf balls, golf clubs, golf bags, apparel, and more. Each multi-functional team included senior executives from marketing, finance, manufacturing, global sourcing, customer service, and sales. All of each team's participants were encouraged to share their honest opinions without any fear of retribution.

Within three months of this fast-tracked turnaround mission, our teams achieved organizational alignment on the Current State and Desired Future State, obstacles to overcome, and initiatives to be launched. It wasn't easy, but the new model and method invigorated the team members to start solving problems that had lurked beneath the surface—apparent to them all, but never defined or agreed upon. We addressed the challenges of choosing where and how to manufacture and sell Wilson products and solved those problems. But more than that, our team also found organizational alignment in the process and applied the same approach to identifying and overcoming other growth-related obstacles.

As a result, Wilson USA Golf experienced explosive financial and market share growth acceleration over the next four years. They were amazing times for the brand and everyone involved. This rapid transformation was a testament to the power of achieving organizational alignment and the effectiveness of a unified, multi-functional team approach.

Through this experience, it became even more evident to me that it is critical to foster open communication and to encourage honest input from all functional areas. No organization I was part of would ever allow lines of communication to be stifled by fear or uncertainty. Communication is key.

ALIGNING THE VISION WITH ORGANIZATIONAL GOALS

Of course, aligning diverse perspectives into a unified vision is easier said than done. It requires a deep understanding of each team member's viewpoint and a willingness to find common ground. Fixing this misalignment is where the real work begins, involving numerous discussions, debates, and compromises. The goal is to create a vision that reflects the aspirations of the entire leadership team and aligns with the organization's broader objectives. This vision should be ambitious yet attainable, embodying the collective ambition of the organization while remaining realistic. It should serve as a guiding star for all future decisions and initiatives, providing a clear framework for action and growth.

In my experience, a strong vision aligns with the organization's core values and long-term goals. It should not only inspire and motivate your team but also provide a clear sense of direction and purpose, fostering a shared commitment to the organization's success. At the same time, it needs to be grounded in reality, reflecting the organization's capabilities and market conditions. This balance between aspiration and practicality is crucial for sustaining momentum and achieving lasting success. A well-crafted vision can unify the team, drive strategic initiatives, and ultimately lead the organization toward its desired future.

A strong vision typically includes several key components:

1. **Clarity and Simplicity:** The vision should be clear and easy to understand. It should articulate what the organization aims to achieve and how it plans to get there.

2. **Alignment with Core Values:** The vision must align with the organization's core values and culture. It should reflect what the organization stands for and what it aspires to be.

3. **Achievable Goals:** While the vision should be ambitious, it must also be realistic and attainable. It should outline

specific, measurable goals that the organization can work toward.

4. **Involvement of Key Stakeholders:** Developing a vision is not a solo endeavor. It requires input and buy-in from key stakeholders across the organization. Their involvement ensures that the vision reflects a collective aspiration and fosters a sense of ownership.

INVOLVEMENT OF KEY STAKEHOLDERS

Engaging key stakeholders in the vision creation process is absolutely essential for ensuring alignment and buy-in across the entire organization. This involves much more than just the leadership team; it also extends to employees at all levels, customers, and even external partners. By involving a broad range of perspectives, you ensure that the vision is both comprehensive and inclusive, capturing diverse viewpoints and insights. This inclusive approach not only fosters a sense of ownership and commitment among all participants but also enhances the overall quality and feasibility of the vision. It encourages open dialogue, promotes innovative thinking, and helps to identify potential challenges and opportunities that might otherwise be overlooked. Ultimately, this collaborative process builds a stronger foundation for the vision, leading to more effective implementation and greater long-term success.

Let's revisit my time at Wilson Sporting Goods. At the beginning our growth acceleration journey, we held a series of workshops involving employees from various departments. These sessions were designed to gather input and ensure that our vision reflected the aspirations of the entire organization. As we proceeded with our multifunctional team meetings, all stakeholders felt like part of our strategic growth turnaround plan. They felt their voices had been heard; they told me so many times over.

They had a sense of ownership, which they enthusiastically passed along their team members, who then also felt "ownership" in the entire Desired Future State turnaround success.

The off-site vision meeting is a collaborative effort in which each leader's vision is revealed and discussed. This is a time for open dialogue and honest feedback. It's about building a shared understanding of where the organization wants to go and how to get there.

During my career at Gillette, we enjoyed year-after-year, non-stop growth acceleration. This success became a textbook case study in growth-acceleration–focused organizational alignment. I attribute this to a powerful mantra that permeated the entire organization, from the CEO and C-suite down to every employee: "Everyone is in sales."

This mantra signified a multi-functional understanding that sales and revenue acceleration are collaborative endeavors. It wasn't just the sales department driving growth; it was a coordinated effort that included finance, marketing, manufacturing, supply chain, R&D, human resources, and sales. Every VP, director, manager, supervisor, and employee embraced this philosophy. The mantra of "Everyone is in sales" was seamlessly integrated into the Annual Operating Performance Plans or Desired Future State (DFS) plans of every functional head and employee.

During this multi-year period of sustained growth acceleration at Gillette, we consistently carried a 34 PE ratio, while the rest of our sector averaged 15. We were referred to as a "Darling of Wall Street." For those of us fortunate enough to be part of this remarkable journey, it was clear that multi-functional team discussions and the resulting "everybody is in sales" collaboration were keys to our success.

Every department understood how its role contributed to sales and growth. Finance ensured that budgets supported growth initiatives. Marketing crafted campaigns that resonated with customers. Manufacturing and supply chain optimized production and delivery. R&D innovated new products that met market demands. Human resources recruited and trained talent to support these efforts. Sales executed strategies with precision. This comprehensive, unified approach created a synergy that drove Gillette's sustained success.

The impact of this alignment was profound. Our sustained success soon attracted aggressive buyout offers, with Gillette finally accepting Procter & Gamble's lucrative M&A proposal. This acquisition was a testament to the power of organizational alignment and the effectiveness of a shared vision where all employees truly believed they were in sales.

Reflecting on this period, I realize that the key to Gillette's success was more than just a powerful mantra. It was about creating a culture where every employee understood his or her role in driving growth and felt empowered to contribute to the company's success. This holistic, multi-functional approach is a model for any organization striving for sustained growth and market leadership.

ONE MORE CASE STUDY

I've seen firsthand the impact of a well-crafted vision.

I was recruited into Alberto Culver to help plan and lead a growth-acceleration mission. There were many similarities between Gillette and Alberto Culver during that period. Both companies were very sales focused. At Alberto Culver, our vision and accompanying mission were to become a top-three leader in health and beauty aids and hair care. This vision was enthusiastically communicated to the entire company by our revered CEO, chairman, and founder, Mr. Leonard Lavin, who I was privileged to have as a personal mentor.

Mr. Lavin was a truly remarkable entrepreneur. He founded Alberto Culver by selling VO5 Hot Oil from the trunk of his car to Hollywood starlets, who felt their delicate hair was being damaged by the bright filming lights. A genius marketer, Mr. Lavin was an original pioneer in using TV advertising's return on investment (ROI) brand-building power. Yet, like the CEO of Gillette during the same period, Mr. Lavin instilled in the entire organization the same mantra: "Everyone is in sales."

This growth-accelerating, multi-functional team philosophy produced extraordinary financial results for Alberto Culver. The mantra signified that sales and revenue acceleration were not the sole responsibility of the sales department but a collaborative effort across all functions. Every department—finance, marketing, manufacturing, supply chain, R&D, human resources, and sales—embraced this philosophy.

Mr. Lavin's leadership and vision created a culture in which every employee understood his or her role in driving growth. This holistic, unified approach ensured that each department worked together seamlessly to achieve our ambitious goals. Finance provided the necessary budgets for growth initiatives. Marketing crafted compelling campaigns that resonated with customers. Manufacturing and supply chain optimized production and delivery. R&D developed new innovative products that met market demands. Human resources recruited and trained talent to support these efforts. Sales executed strategies with precision.

The result of this cohesive approach was remarkable. Alberto Culver's sustained growth and market leadership attracted a lucrative multi-billion dollar purchase from Unilever. This acquisition was a testament to the power of organizational alignment and the effectiveness of a shared vision in which all employees truly believed they were in sales.

Reflecting on my time at Alberto Culver, I realize that the key to our success was more than just a powerful mantra. It fostered a culture in which every employee felt empowered to contribute to the company's success. This multi-functional team philosophy not only drove growth but also created an environment where innovation and collaboration thrived.

The lessons learned from my time at Alberto Culver reinforced the importance of a unified vision and the power of a collaborative, growth-focused culture. These principles are essential for any organization aiming to achieve sustained growth and market leadership.

CONCLUSION: THE PATH TO A UNIFIED VISION

Defining the desired future state is a critical step in the transformation journey. It will provide a clear direction and a sense of purpose that will guide your organization's efforts. By engaging key stakeholders, fostering open dialogue, and aligning diverse perspectives, you can create a vision that inspires and unites your team.

As we move forward, this vision will serve as our guiding star, helping us navigate the challenges and opportunities that lie ahead. In the next chapter, we will begin to develop a strategic roadmap that will bridge the gap between our current state and our desired future state, setting us on a path to sustainable growth and success.

4

CREATING A ROADMAP FOR TRANSFORMATION

Interactive Video Chapter Summary

Or text **roadmap** to 855-426-7770

By scanning this QR code and sending the keyword you are consenting to join the author's SMS loyalty program. We do not share your data with third parties. Msg&Data Rates May Apply. Msg Freq Varies. Send HELP for help, reply STOP to 855.426.7770 to end.

—ɯ—

Y ou've assessed your Current State by
soliciting feedback from your organization and possibly from a few impartial third
parties. You did this carefully and without
pushing back against anyone's observations.

Then you defined your Desired Future State
by asking your department heads for three-bul-
let-point summaries of where they want their
departments to be at the end of your organization's growth transformation process. You did
this at an off-site meeting where each department head presented his or her bullet points
for discussion and further development.

Now it's time to develop a comprehensive
and actionable **Strategic Plan** that will guide
your organization toward its future goals.

This is where the rubber meets the road.
Crafting your Strategic Plan is about turning
aspirations into reality by outlining the steps
your team will take, setting the goals you need

to achieve, and defining the initiatives necessary to bridge the gap between your Current State and your Desired Future State. This plan serves as a roadmap, detailing the specific actions and strategies needed to achieve your long-term vision.

Creating a Strategic Plan involves setting clear, achievable goals and identifying the key initiatives required to reach them. This process should be inclusive, involving input from various departments to ensure that the plan is comprehensive and aligned with the organization's vision. It should also consider potential challenges and opportunities, allowing for flexibility and adjustments as needed. By engaging stakeholders from different areas of the organization, you can ensure that the plan is not only well-rounded but also has the support needed for successful implementation.

Additionally, it is crucial to establish metrics and benchmarks to track progress and measure success. Regular reviews and updates to the plan can help keep the organization on track and responsive to any changes in the internal or external environment. With a well-thought-out strategic plan, your organization can confidently move forward, knowing that it has a clear path to achieving its aspirations.

SETTING SMART GOALS

One of the most important aspects of creating a comprehensive and effective roadmap is setting SMART goals. These serve as a foundational guide to keep your project on track and ensure that all team members are aligned. They have particular characteristics that make them unique and always aligned with pushing your organization toward your Desired Future State. There are some different variations of this method. But in my book, SMART goals are characterized by the following criteria:

- **Specific:** Clearly define what you want to achieve in precise terms. A specific goal provides a clear direction and avoids any ambiguity, making it easier for everyone involved to understand the objective. For example, instead of saying, "I want to increase sales," specify "I want to increase sales by 20 percent within the next six months through online marketing strategies and customer outreach programs." This not only sets a clear target but also outlines a potential method for achieving it, ensuring that all team members are on the same page and can work together effectively toward the common goal.

- **Measurable:** Ensure that you can track progress and measure success using quantifiable criteria. Measurable goals enable you to monitor your progress and make necessary adjustments along the way to stay on course. By establishing clear metrics and benchmarks, you can objectively assess how well you are doing at each stage. This allows for a more precise understanding of what is working and what needs improvement, ensuring that your efforts are aligned with your overall objectives.

- **Achievable:** It is important to set realistic and attainable goals that take into account your resources and any possible constraints. By establishing achievable goals, you can motivate your team members to strive for success without overwhelming them. These goals should be challenging enough to inspire effort and innovation, yet they should be attainable to avoid causing frustration and burnout. The balance between challenge and attainability is crucial for maintaining team morale and ensuring steady progress toward your objectives.

- **Relevant:** Align goals with the organization's vision and objectives. Relevant goals ensure that every effort contributes to the broader mission of the organization, making sure that resources are used effectively and efficiently. By establishing relevant goals, teams can focus on what truly matters. This alignment helps in prioritizing tasks and projects that will have the most significant impact on the organization's success. Relevant goals serve as a guiding compass, helping to navigate through challenges and opportunities while staying true to the organization's core values and long-term aspirations.

- **Time-bound:** Establish a clear timeline for achieving each goal. Time-bound goals create a sense of urgency and help prioritize tasks, ensuring that milestones are met and the project progresses steadily. By setting specific deadlines, you can monitor progress more effectively and make adjustments as needed to stay on track. Additionally, having a defined timeframe encourages accountability and motivates team members to stay focused and committed to achieving the objectives within the set period.

That's it.

By adhering to these SMART goals, you will create a structured, focused, and efficient roadmap for your team. I've seen it happen time and again. Sticking to this method religiously will significantly increase the likelihood of your organization reaching, and maybe even surpassing, your Desired Future State.

But remember, effective transformation requires collaboration across all of your organization's departments to ensure that everyone is aligned and working toward the same objectives. This collaborative effort is essential for setting SMART goals, and it is just as crucial as undertaking any other initiatives or strategies we've discussed so far. By fostering open communication and teamwork, you can ensure that employees in every department understand their roles and contributions, ultimately driving the organization toward successful transformation.

Throughout your growth acceleration journey, each department must play a role in implementing the strategic plan. Efforts need to be coordinated between departments to ensure alignment and avoid wasted energy and duplication of effort. This kind of cross-departmental collaboration fosters a sense of shared purpose and helps to break down silos that can, and will, hinder progress. From Gillette to Wilson Sporting Goods to Alberto Culver, I've witnessed firsthand the power of genuine collaboration. This kind of synergy can take time to figure out, but it works magic once everyone is on board.

PRACTICAL STEPS FOR PLAN DEVELOPMENT

Developing a strategic plan involves several practical steps that are essential for ensuring the success and alignment of your organization's goals:

1. **Identify Key Stakeholders:** Begin by determining who needs to be involved in the planning process. This includes

department heads, key team members, and external advisors if necessary. It's crucial to ensure that all relevant parties are included to provide diverse perspectives and expertise.

2. **Conduct a SWOT Analysis:** Take the time to evaluate your organization's strengths, weaknesses, opportunities, and threats. This analysis will help you identify key areas for improvement and growth. By understanding your internal and external environment, you can make informed decisions and strategic choices.

3. **Set SMART Goals:** Define specific, measurable, achievable, relevant, and time-bound goals that align with your vision. These goals should be clear and concise to provide a roadmap for your organization's future success. Ensure that each goal is realistic and attainable within the given timeframe.

4. **Define Key Initiatives:** Identify the actions and projects that will drive progress toward your goals. These initiatives should be well-planned and prioritized based on their potential impact.

Consider breaking down larger projects into smaller, manageable tasks to maintain momentum.

5. **Create a Timeline:** Establish a detailed timeline for each initiative, with milestones and deadlines to track progress. A well-structured timeline helps in monitoring the advancement of each project and ensures that everything stays on schedule. Regularly review and adjust the timeline as needed to accommodate changes and unforeseen challenges.

6. **Assign Responsibilities:** Clearly define who is responsible for each initiative and ensure that the necessary resources and support are available to succeed. Assigning responsibilities helps in accountability and ensures that everyone knows his or her role in the strategic plan. Provide training and resources to empower your team members to achieve their tasks effectively.

7. **Develop a Communication Plan:** Ensure that all members of the organization understand the strategic plan and their roles in achieving it. Communication is key to maintaining

alignment and momentum. Regular updates, meetings, and feedback sessions are essential to keep everyone informed and engaged. Foster an environment where open communication is encouraged and valued.

By following these steps, you can create a comprehensive and effective strategic plan that guides your organization toward its goals and objectives.

EXAMPLES OF EFFECTIVE STRATEGIC PLANS

My experience as senior vice president at Brunswick focused on "turn-around-growth-acceleration," and it stands out as one of the highlights of my career. Our team's success was rooted in the development and execution of a highly controversial and intricately complex "Cross-Channel" plan. Let me take you through it.

Brunswick, renowned for its premium boating products and Mercury Marine engines, sought to diversify into outdoor recreation beyond boating. As part of this strategy, the company acquired several sports and recreation businesses, including Roadmaster Bicycle Company and Service Cycle, the latter known for its marquee but underperforming brand, Mongoose, which specialized in BMX bicycles.

Soon after these acquisitions, global trade and tariff laws shifted, unexpectedly allowing Chinese manufacturers to aggressively enter the U.S. bicycle market. The $230 million Roadmaster unit, based in Olney, Illinois, faced a dire situation. With higher production costs in the U.S., Roadmaster couldn't compete against the lower-cost Chinese imports. Upon my arrival as SVP, my team conducted a thorough revenue forecast to assess the impact. The results were staggering: the $230 million forecast for Roadmaster plummeted to a mere $120 million, as retailers dropped the brand due to uncompetitive pricing and outdated designs. The Chinese factories not only had significantly lower production costs but also offered more advanced aluminum frames and welding.

Faced with this potential financial disaster, we devised a bold strategic response. We decided to reposition the upscale, boutique Mongoose brand, previously sold in specialty shops, into the mass market, targeting such major retailers as Walmart, Target, Best Buy, and Dick's

Sporting Goods. This move was unprecedented in the bicycle industry; no specialty shop brand had ever dared to cross channels. But we were determined to succeed despite the risks.

This shift required a cohesive organizational alignment across all functional areas of Brunswick's Bicycles Division. The stakes were high, and the pressure was intense. There was a real fear that specialty shop dealers would boycott Mongoose once they learned of the cross-channel strategy. Moreover, if the mass retailers didn't fully commit to Mongoose, the expected revenue from these channels wouldn't compensate for the losses in the specialty market.

To navigate these challenges, we launched an ultra-premium line of Mongoose road and mountain bikes, priced from $499 to $5,000, exclusively for specialty shops. We also formed a world-famous Mongoose Cycles Racing Team, featuring both male and female athletes, to enhance the brand's prestige. To promote the new high-end Mongoose brand, we engineered the industry's largest trade-show booth and made a grand impression at the Atlanta Sporting Goods Super Show with cocktail parties and press conferences. Our goal was to position Mongoose at the pinnacle of the brand image pyramid.

Once we established this premium image, we initiated discussions with the major retailers, who were eager to carry the brand. This strategic pivot transformed a potential financial disaster into a success story. It required shifting much of our production to Southeast Asia, building new global supply chains, and integrating new teams of product developers, marketers, and national account managers who were comfortable working with both mass retailers and specialty shops.

The result was groundbreaking: we became the first cycling company to offer top-quality, stylish products to mass retailers, making high-end bicycles accessible to all U.S. consumers. The two-year process of merging Mongoose and Roadmaster, deploying the cross-channel strategy, and anchoring the brand at the top of the market image pyramid made Brunswick a hot commodity in the cycling industry. Mongoose, in particular, became a sensation, allowing us to expand into accessories, apparel, snowboarding, and rollerblading. We garnered significant media attention, won two Product of the Year awards, and saw our revenue projections soar.

Initially, the post-acquisition forecast for Roadmaster had dropped from $230 million to $120 million, with Mongoose stagnating at around $25 million. By the end of the two-year cross-channel strategy, the forecast had risen to $250–$275 million. This success enabled Brunswick to spin off the Bicycle Division and return to its core boating business.

Overcoming the many functional challenges of this unprecedented and controversial pivot required relentless focus on organizational alignment and a clear mission to achieve the desired future state. Much of the credit goes to our president, Dave L., a transformative visionary who provided the necessary mission, vision, and support across financial, marketing, PR, and sales functions.

TOOLS FOR PLANNING AND EXECUTION

A wide variety of tools is available to assist individuals and organizations in both strategic planning and execution. These tools are designed to simplify complex processes, provide structure, and ensure that all critical aspects of planning are addressed effectively. Some of the tools I've found most useful in my experience include:

- **Gantt Charts:** These are excellent tools for visualizing timelines and tracking progress over the course of a project. By displaying tasks along a timeline, Gantt charts help ensure that everyone on the team understands the overall project schedule, key milestones, and responsibilities. This visual representation also aids in identifying potential bottlenecks and dependencies between tasks, making it easier to adjust plans and allocate resources more effectively. Gantt charts foster better communication and coordination among team members, contributing to the successful completion of the project.

- **Project Management Software:** Tools such as Asana, Trello, and Microsoft Project are essential for managing tasks effectively. These tools not only help in assigning responsibilities to team members but also play a crucial role in monitoring progress throughout the project lifecycle. They offer various features such as task scheduling, deadline tracking, and real-time collaboration, which are invaluable for keeping everyone on track. By using these tools, teams can ensure that projects are completed on time, within scope, and to the desired quality standards. Additionally, they provide transparency and accountability, making it easier to identify and address any issues that may arise during the project.

- **Balanced Scorecards:** This valuable tool helps an organization track its performance against strategic goals by providing detailed metrics and comprehensive analysis. By offering a well-rounded view of various performance indicators, it allows management to understand how the organization is progressing in multiple areas. Additionally, it highlights specific areas that need attention, enabling leaders to make informed decisions and take corrective actions to ensure the organization stays on track to achieve its objectives.

Remember, no matter what tools you use, creating a strategic plan is not a one-time event. It's an ongoing process that requires continual review and adaptation. Regularly review your progress against the plan, assess what's working and what's not, and make adjustments as needed. This ensures that your plan remains relevant and effective in the face of changing circumstances.

Additionally, it's important to involve key stakeholders in the review process to gain diverse perspectives and insights. Regular meetings and check-ins can help keep everyone aligned and informed about the plan's progress and any necessary changes. Keep in mind that flexibility and openness to feedback are crucial for the success of your strategic plan. By doing so, you ensure that your organization remains agile and capable of responding proactively to any challenges or opportunities that may arise.

CONCLUSION: THE ROADMAP TO SUCCESS

Creating a roadmap for transformation is about more than just setting goals; it's about developing a comprehensive, actionable plan that guides your organization toward its desired future state. This involves a meticulous process where every aspect of the organization's operations is considered and aligned with the overall objectives. By setting SMART (Specific, Measurable, Achievable, Relevant, and Time-bound) goals, defining key initiatives that drive progress, fostering cross-departmental collaboration to ensure all parts of the organization are working in harmony, and continually reviewing and adapting your plan to reflect new insights and changing circumstances, you can navigate the complex challenges of transformation and achieve lasting success. This holistic approach ensures that every step taken is purposeful and contributes meaningfully to the overarching vision.

As we move forward, the next chapter will focus on overcoming the obstacles and challenges that are an inevitable part of any transformation journey. We'll explore in-depth strategies for dealing with resistance to change, which often stems from a reluctance to move away from established routines. Additionally, we will address resource constraints, including budget limitations and manpower shortages, and how to creatively manage these limitations to maintain momentum. Other common hurdles, such as aligning short-term actions with long-term goals and maintaining stakeholder engagement, will also be discussed. By understanding and preparing for these challenges, we set the stage for successful implementation and long-term growth, ensuring that the transformation is not only achieved but also sustained over time.

5

OVERCOMING OBSTACLES AND CHALLENGES

Interactive Video Chapter Summary

Or text **overcome** to 855-426-7770

I t's like clockwork.

Embarking on a transformation journey brings obstacles to the surface. Some of them you will be prepared for, and others you won't. These challenges can appear suddenly and without warning, catching you off guard and testing your resilience and adaptability.

But you can be sure that no matter where you are or what you're doing, obstacles will show up. It's an iron law of business (and of life in general). Whether you are launching a new product, entering a new market, or simply trying to improve your current operations, difficulties will inevitably arise.

This chapter is about my experiences and insights on how to navigate challenges and overcome obstacles. The key is this: Overcoming obstacles isn't just about addressing problems as they arise, but about anticipating potential issues with an eye toward the future. It involves carefully preparing your team to address specific challenges in ways that work to their existing strengths. Additionally, it's about creating a culture that embraces and even welcomes change—a team that expects hard things to happen along the way. This proactive approach ensures that when challenges do appear, your team is ready to tackle them head-on with confidence and competence. By fostering a resilient mindset and a forward-thinking attitude, you can turn potential setbacks into opportunities for growth and improvement.

COMMON OBSTACLES IN THE TRANSFORMATION PROCESS

Transformational change often brings to light several common obstacles. Recognizing these challenges early on can help you develop strategies to address them proactively. Here are some of the most frequent obstacles I've encountered:

1. **Resistance to Change:** People are naturally resistant to change, especially when it disrupts a routine or challenges one's comfort zone. This resistance can manifest as passive reluctance,

active opposition, or even sabotage. Overcoming this resistance requires effective communication, empathy, and sometimes even incentivizing the change to make it more appealing.

2. **Resource Constraints:** Limited resources, including time, money, and personnel, can hinder the implementation of your transformation plan. Balancing the demands of day-to-day operations with the needs of the transformation process is often a significant challenge. It may be necessary to prioritize certain initiatives or seek additional funding and support to ensure the transformation can proceed smoothly.

3. **Lack of Alignment:** Misalignment between departments or within the leadership team can create friction and impede progress. Ensuring that everyone is on the same page and working toward the same goals is crucial for success. Regular meetings, clear communication, and a unified vision can help bridge gaps and foster a collaborative environment.

4. **Inadequate Skills or Capabilities:** Transformation may require new skills or capabilities that your organization currently lacks. Identifying and addressing these gaps is essential for moving forward. This might involve hiring new talent, upskilling current employees, or bringing in external consultants who specialize in the areas where the organization is lacking.

5. **Cultural Barriers:** Organizational culture can be a powerful force for or against change. Cultural barriers, such as a lack of trust or a fear of failure, can significantly impact the success of your transformation efforts. Building a culture that embraces change involves fostering open communication, encouraging risk-taking, and celebrating small wins to build momentum for larger changes.

STRATEGIES FOR OVERCOMING OBSTACLES

To navigate these challenges effectively, it's essential to adopt a proactive approach and equip yourself with a range of effective strategies. Here are some methods that have proven successful in my experience and can be highly beneficial:

1. *Communication: The Key to Managing Resistance*

   Effective communication is critical in overcoming resistance to change. People need to understand the reasons for the change, how it will affect them, and the benefits it will bring. Communicate openly and honestly about the transformation process, addressing any concerns or fears that may arise. This transparent approach can help in building trust and reducing apprehension.

2. *Training and Development: Bridging the Skills Gap*

   Transformation often requires new skills and capabilities. Providing training and development opportunities for your team is essential to ensure they have the skills needed to succeed in the new environment. Invest in upskilling your workforce and providing the support they need to adapt to new roles and responsibilities. Continual learning and development initiatives can significantly enhance the adaptability of your team, ensuring they are well prepared for future challenges.

3. *Resource Management: Balancing Competing Demands*

Resource constraints are common obstacles in the transformation process. Effective resource management involves prioritizing initiatives, allocating resources wisely, and ensuring that your team members have the tools and support they need to succeed. It's about finding a balance between maintaining daily operations and driving transformation. This might include conducting regular resource assessments to identify gaps and reallocating resources to high-priority projects to maximize efficiency and impact.

4. *Building Alignment: Creating a Unified Team*

Misalignment can derail your transformation efforts. It's crucial to ensure that everyone in the organization, from the leadership team to front-line employees, is aligned with the vision and committed to achieving the goals. This involves fostering a sense of shared purpose and creating a culture of collaboration and accountability. Regularly communicating the vision and progress toward goals can help maintain alignment and keep the team motivated and focused.

5. *Cultural Change: Fostering a Culture of Innovation and Adaptability*

Cultural barriers can be some of the most challenging obstacles to overcome. Transforming an organization's culture involves creating an environment that encourages innovation, embraces change, and supports risk-taking. This requires strong leadership and a commitment to fostering a positive, forward-thinking culture. Implementing initiatives that reward innovative thinking and celebrating successes can gradually shift the organizational mindset toward one that is more adaptable and open to change.

CASE STUDY: ADDRESSING RESOURCE CONSTRAINTS AT DIDGEBRIDGE

In my current role as CEO and co-founder of Didgebridge, we face a significant challenge: convincing marketers that Public Internet Web2.0 marketing is fundamentally flawed regarding data privacy, trust, and ROI metrics. We emphasize that all communication flowing through Web2.0 is susceptible to mining, harvesting, and even weaponization against the marketer. The core issue lies in the very nature of Web2.0, designed from its inception to be a public, collaborative space where everyone is interconnected. This openness, as articulated by Mark Zuckerberg, also means that sensitive and costly marketing data, including web-based leads and engagements, are vulnerable to being mined, shared, and retargeted by competitors.

To illustrate, consider the scene from the movie *Glengarry Glen Ross* in which Jack Lemmon's character desperately pleads with his boss, played by Kevin Spacey, for the "good leads." This scene underscores the crucial role of proprietary leads in sales success. In the digital marketing world, these leads translate into such metrics as clicks, page views, time-on-page, and app downloads. Unfortunately, $84 billion worth of these so-called engagement metrics are often fraudulent, generated by bots rather than real humans. Over the past twenty-five years, the marketing industry has become complacent, accepting that the only way to operate is through Web2.0's mega-platform companies, which manipulate ROI metrics and hijack digital leads, reselling them to competitors. This ethically questionable business model of "Big-Tech-Marketing-Platform" companies undermines data privacy, trust, and ROI metrics in Web2.0 digital marketing.

To address this glaring issue, we at Didgebridge have developed a solution: the Intellismart Marketing Platform. Intellismart leverages mobile-SMS-telecom to ensure that only real humans, not bots, can make private one-on-one connections. These interactions generate proprietary Web3.1 web pages, completely outside the Web2.0 data-minable communication ecosystem. As a result, the hard-earned leads and engagements of marketers remain private and are not resold to competitors, unlike what has happened in the Web2.0 marketing environment for over two decades.

For a practical demonstration, you can see an example of Intellismart's deployment with P&G/CVS by scanning the QR code or texting the number provided below. Stay tuned for my upcoming book on the *Web2.0 Privacy, Trust, and ROI Challenge—and related solutions*, where I will delve deeper into these issues and our innovative solutions.

THE ROLE OF LEADERSHIP IN NAVIGATING OBSTACLES

As a leader, your role in navigating obstacles is critical. You need to be a proactive problem solver, adept at identifying potential issues before they escalate and implementing effective solutions swiftly. Furthermore, being a clear communicator is essential; you must ensure that your team members are well-informed and understand the direction and goals of the organization. Additionally, you must be a consistent source of support and inspiration for them, motivating them and fostering a positive and productive work environment. It's your responsibility to create an environment where challenges are viewed not as setbacks but as opportunities for growth and innovation, encouraging your team to think creatively and push boundaries.

Leadership is about more than just managing tasks; it involves guiding your team members through uncertainty, providing the vision and tools they need to succeed, and helping them overcome the inevitable challenges that arise during periods of transformation. This means being resilient, adaptable, and open to new ideas and approaches. Your ability to navigate these obstacles effectively and with confidence will determine the overall success of your transformation efforts. By demonstrating strong leadership qualities, you can inspire trust and loyalty among your team members, ensuring that everyone remains committed and aligned with the organizational goals.

CONCLUSION: EMBRACING CHALLENGES AS OPPORTUNITIES

Overcoming obstacles is an integral part of any transformation journey. By anticipating potential challenges, communicating effectively, providing the necessary training and resources, and fostering a positive organizational culture, you can navigate these obstacles successfully. Remember, every challenge is an opportunity to learn, grow, and improve. By embracing these opportunities and leading with resilience and determination, you can guide your organization toward a successful transformation and a brighter future.

In the next chapter, we will explore the implementation phase of the transformation journey, focusing on change management techniques, maintaining momentum, and tracking progress. This is where the plans we've developed come to life and the real work of transformation begins.

6

IMPLEMENTATION AND CHANGE MANAGEMENT

Interactive Video Chapter Summary

Or text **transform** to 855-426-7770

C reating a vision and developing a strategic plan are pivotal steps in your organization's transformation journey. We've established that much. Crafting a clear and compelling vision provides direction, while a well-thought-out strategic plan offers a roadmap for achieving your goals.

These steps are essential, but they are just the beginning of a much larger process.

But the real test of your leadership lies in the implementation phase—where ideas and plans are put into action. This is where the true challenge arises, as the transition from theory to practice often reveals unforeseen obstacles and complexities.

Anyone can talk a big game. Believe me; I've seen hundreds of people do it. They have big ideas and master plans on paper. But when the rubber hits the road, they fall flat. They expect others to make things happen. They wonder why outlining their vision and their plan didn't just make magic happen—they refuse to believe that it's on them not only to tell people what needs to be done, but also to get down in the mud to help them do those things. Real leadership requires more than just eloquent speeches and detailed documents; it demands active participation and a willingness to lead by example.

This chapter is about how to implement your transformation plan, manage change, and maintain the momentum needed to achieve lasting success. Implementation is the hard part. It involves rallying your team, continually communicating your vision, and overcoming resistance to change. The ability to adapt and respond to challenges as they arise is crucial. This chapter will provide you with practical strategies and insights to guide you through the implementation process, ensuring that your vision is not only realized but also sustained over time.

THE CHALLENGE OF IMPLEMENTATION

Implementing a transformation plan can often feel like navigating uncharted waters. It's a complex, dynamic process that requires careful coordination, clear communication, and unwavering commitment. The success of this phase depends on your ability to translate high-level strategies into concrete actions that drive the organization toward its desired future state.

It's easy to underestimate the complexity of this phase. You might have a detailed plan in place, but executing that plan requires agility and resilience. You'll need to adapt to unforeseen challenges, manage competing priorities, and keep your team motivated and aligned. This chapter will guide you through the key elements of successful implementation and change management.

DEVELOPING A DETAILED ACTION PLAN

A successful implementation begins with a detailed action plan. This plan serves as a roadmap, outlining the steps, timelines, and responsibilities required to achieve your goals. It's essential to break down your strategic initiatives into manageable tasks, each with clear objectives and deadlines. This approach ensures that all team members understand their roles in the transformation and how their efforts contribute to the overall vision.

Creating this plan involves more than just listing tasks. It's about defining the specific actions needed to bridge the gap between your current state and your desired future state. This may include changes to processes, the introduction of new technologies, or shifts in organizational structure. Each action should be clearly defined, with measurable outcomes that allow you to track progress and make adjustments as needed.

ASSIGNING RESPONSIBILITIES AND ENSURING ACCOUNTABILITY

Clear accountability is crucial for successful implementation. Each initiative should have a designated owner responsible for driving it forward and ensuring its completion. This individual accountability helps maintain focus and ensures that tasks don't fall through the cracks. It also fosters a sense of ownership and commitment, motivating team members to contribute actively to the transformation.

Accountability should be embedded in your organizational culture. It's about creating an environment where people feel responsible for their work and are motivated to achieve their goals. This requires setting clear expectations, providing regular feedback, and recognizing individual contributions. By fostering a culture of accountability, you can ensure that everyone in the organization is working toward the same objectives.

COMMUNICATING EFFECTIVELY

Effective communication is the lifeblood of successful implementation. It ensures that everyone in the organization understands the plan, his or her role in it, and how each individual's work contributes to the overall goals. Regular updates and open channels of communication help keep everyone informed, engaged, and aligned with the transformation objectives.

Communication should be clear, consistent, and inclusive. It's about keeping your team informed of progress, celebrating successes, and addressing challenges openly. This helps build trust and ensures that everyone is on the same page. It also provides an opportunity for feedback and input, allowing you to make adjustments and improvements as needed.

MONITORING PROGRESS AND ADAPTING

Implementation is not a static process; it requires regular monitoring and adaptation. Regularly review your progress against the plan, identify any issues or obstacles, and make necessary adjustments to stay on track. This iterative approach helps ensure that your implementation efforts remain aligned with your goals and can adapt to changing circumstances.

Monitoring progress involves more than just tracking metrics. It's about understanding the impact of your actions and identifying areas where adjustments are needed. This may involve revisiting your plan, reallocating resources, or changing your approach to address new challenges. By staying flexible and responsive, you can ensure that your implementation efforts remain effective and relevant.

CHANGE MANAGEMENT: GUIDING YOUR TEAM THROUGH TRANSITION

Effective change management is critical to the success of any transformation. It involves helping your team to adapt to new ways of working and to embrace the changes needed to achieve your vision. Change can be challenging, but with the right approach, you can turn it into an opportunity for growth and innovation.

Change management starts with a clear understanding of the impact of the transformation on your team. It's about identifying the changes that will occur, understanding how they will affect your employees, and developing strategies to help them adapt. This may involve training, support, and communication to ensure that everyone understands the reasons for the change and feels prepared to embrace it.

One of the most important aspects of change management is building trust. Your team members need to feel confident that the changes are in their best interests and that they have the support they need to succeed. This involves being transparent about the reasons for the change, providing regular updates, and being available to answer questions and address concerns.

ENGAGING AND EMPOWERING YOUR TEAM

Engaging and empowering your team is absolutely essential for successful change management. This involves actively involving your employees in the change process from the very beginning, seeking their valuable input on decisions, and providing numerous opportunities for them to take full ownership of the changes being implemented. By involving your team in these crucial steps, you can effectively build buy-in and significantly reduce any resistance to change that might arise.

Additionally, empowering your team members also means providing them with all the necessary tools and resources they need to succeed. This may involve comprehensive training programs to help them develop new skills, access to cutting-edge technologies that can facilitate their work, or ongoing support so they can seamlessly navigate through the changes. By empowering your employees in this manner, you can ensure that they feel not only confident but also fully capable of achieving their goals and contributing positively to the organization.

Moreover, creating an environment where team members feel valued and heard can foster a sense of belonging and loyalty, further enhancing their commitment to the change initiatives. Regularly communicating the vision and benefits of the changes can also help in maintaining their motivation and alignment with the overall objectives. By taking these additional steps, you can build a resilient team that is well-prepared to handle future challenges and drive sustained success.

FOSTERING A CULTURE OF CONTINUAL IMPROVEMENT

A culture of continual improvement is critical for sustaining the momentum of your transformation. It involves encouraging your team to always seek ways to improve processes, products, and outcomes. This culture supports ongoing transformation and helps ensure that your organization remains agile and competitive in a rapidly changing market landscape. By embedding a mindset of continual enhancement, your organization can more effectively respond to emerging challenges and seize new opportunities.

Fostering a culture of continual improvement requires a commitment to learning and growth. It's about creating an environment in which people feel encouraged to take risks, experiment with new ideas, and learn from their experiences. This involves not only providing opportunities for learning and development but also actively promoting a mindset that values curiosity and innovation. Recognizing and rewarding innovation will encourage enthusiasm and commitment among team members. Additionally, it's important to create a supportive environment where people feel valued and motivated, knowing that their contributions are making a difference. Encouraging open communication, providing constructive feedback, and celebrating successes, no matter how small, can further reinforce a culture of continual improvement.

TRACKING PROGRESS AND MAINTAINING MOMENTUM

Maintaining momentum is crucial for the success of your transformation. It's about keeping your team motivated and engaged, tracking progress, and celebrating successes. Regularly review your progress against your goals, identify areas for improvement, and make adjustments as needed. This review process ensures that everyone remains aligned with the overall vision and objectives, fostering a shared sense of accomplishment and direction.

Tracking progress involves more than just measuring outcomes. It's about understanding the impact of your actions and identifying areas where adjustments are needed. This may involve revisiting your plan, reallocating resources, or changing your approach to address new challenges. By staying flexible and responsive, you can ensure that your implementation efforts remain effective and relevant. Additionally, tracking progress helps you recognize the contributions of individual team members, which can further boost morale and commitment to the project. Regular check-ins and updates can also serve as a platform for feedback, allowing for the continual improvement of strategies and methods.

By maintaining this adaptive approach, you create a dynamic environment where your team can thrive and your transformation goals can be achieved with greater efficiency and effectiveness.

CELEBRATING SUCCESS AND RECOGNIZING ACHIEVEMENT

Celebrating success and recognizing achievement are critical for maintaining momentum and keeping your team motivated. Acknowledge the hard work and contributions of your team members and celebrate milestones along the way. This recognition helps build morale and reinforces the importance of the transformation.

Celebrating success is about more than just recognizing individual achievements. It's about acknowledging the collective efforts of your team and celebrating the progress you've made toward your goals. This helps build a sense of accomplishment and motivates your team to continue working toward the transformation.

ADDRESSING CHALLENGES AND OVERCOMING OBSTACLES

Addressing challenges and overcoming obstacles are essential for maintaining momentum and achieving your goals. Identify any issues that arise, address them promptly, and provide the necessary support to overcome them. This proactive approach helps keep the transformation on track and prevents small issues from becoming major roadblocks.

Overcoming obstacles requires a flexible and responsive approach. It's about identifying challenges early, developing strategies to address them, and providing the necessary support to help your team succeed. By staying focused and proactive, you can ensure that your transformation efforts remain on track and achieve the desired outcomes.

CONCLUSION: BRINGING YOUR VISION TO LIFE

Implementing a transformation plan is a complex and challenging process, but with the right strategies and a proactive approach, it can be highly successful. By developing a detailed action plan, assigning responsibilities, communicating effectively, and fostering a culture of continual improvement, you can bring your vision to life and achieve your transformation goals.

In the next chapter, we will focus on measuring success and continual improvement, exploring the metrics and KPIs needed to track progress and the strategies for ensuring that your organization continues to evolve and thrive in a rapidly changing environment.

7

MEASURING SUCCESS AND CONTINUAL IMPROVEMENT

Interactive Video Chapter Summary

Or text **success** to 855-426-7770

As we approach the final stages of our transformation journey, it's crucial to shift our focus to measuring success and fostering a culture of continual improvement. This chapter is dedicated to understanding how to track the progress of your transformation efforts, evaluate their impact, and ensure that your organization remains agile and responsive to change.

Measurement is not just about numbers and metrics; it's about understanding the broader impact of your actions and ensuring that you are on the right path toward your desired future state. It's about learning from your experiences, making informed decisions, and continually striving for improvement.

IMPORTANCE OF METRICS AND KPIS

Metrics and KPIs are essential tools for measuring success in any organization or business. These tools provide a clear and objective way to track progress over time, evaluate outcomes against set goals, and identify specific areas that need improvement. By using the right metrics, you can gain a comprehensive understanding of whether you are achieving your objectives, pinpoint where adjustments are necessary, and discover how you can optimize your efforts moving forward for better results.

When selecting metrics and KPIs, it's crucial to choose those that align closely with your strategic goals and provide meaningful insights into your organization's performance. These metrics should be specific, ensuring that they accurately capture the data you need; measurable, allowing you to track progress quantitatively; and relevant, relating directly to the outcomes you aim to achieve. This alignment allows you to monitor progress effectively and make informed, data-driven decisions. Furthermore, these metrics should be dynamic, capable of evolving as your organization grows and changes, to continually reflect the most pertinent information and adapt to new challenges and opportunities.

In addition to being aligned with strategic goals, the selected metrics and KPIs should be communicated clearly across all levels of the organization. This ensures that everyone understands the key performance indicators and how individual efforts contribute to the overall success. Regularly reviewing and updating these metrics can foster a culture of continual improvement and agility, enabling your organization to respond swiftly to changes in the market or operational environment. By integrating these principles into your performance measurement framework, you can create a robust system that drives sustained growth and success.

DEVELOPING A COMPREHENSIVE MEASUREMENT SYSTEM

To effectively measure success, you need a comprehensive measurement system that integrates various metrics and KPIs across different levels of the organization. This system should provide a holistic view of your performance, capturing both quantitative and qualitative data. It should also be flexible, allowing you to adapt to changing circumstances and continually refine your approach. By having a flexible system, you can ensure that your measurement strategies remain relevant and effective even as market conditions evolve.

A comprehensive measurement system involves more than just tracking individual metrics. It's about understanding the relationships between different metrics and how they contribute to your overall goals. This requires a balanced approach that includes financial metrics, operational metrics, and customer satisfaction metrics, among others. Additionally, this system should be able to highlight the interdependencies between various metrics, offering insights into how improvements in one area might positively impact another. This deeper understanding can help in making more informed decisions and driving better outcomes.

Moreover, incorporating real-time data analytics into your measurement system can greatly enhance its effectiveness. Real-time analytics allow you to continually monitor performance, providing immediate feedback and enabling quicker adjustments. This proactive approach ensures that potential issues are identified and addressed promptly, minimizing their impact on your overall performance.

In summary, developing a comprehensive measurement system is crucial for achieving sustained success. It should be an integrated, flexible, and balanced approach that leverages both quantitative and qualitative data. By understanding the interplay between various metrics and incorporating real-time analytics, you can create a robust framework that supports continual improvement and strategic decision-making.

FINANCIAL METRICS

Financial metrics are critical for understanding the economic impact of your transformation efforts. They provide essential insights into your organization's overall financial health and help you evaluate the ROI of your various initiatives. Key financial metrics may include revenue growth, profit margins, cost savings, and return on assets. These metrics offer a comprehensive view of how your organization is performing financially.

Tracking financial metrics is crucial, as it helps ensure that your transformation efforts are driving sustainable growth and profitability. It also provides a solid basis for making informed financial decisions, such as allocating resources effectively and investing in new initiatives that promise significant returns. By regularly reviewing and analyzing your financial metrics, you can identify emerging trends, understand underlying issues, and make necessary adjustments to optimize your financial performance.

Furthermore, financial metrics serve as a communication tool, allowing you to articulate the financial benefits of your transformation efforts to stakeholders, including investors, employees, and board members. This transparency fosters trust and supports the strategic planning process. Additionally, understanding these metrics can help you benchmark your performance against industry standards, offering a clearer picture of where your organization stands relative to competitors.

Ultimately, a thorough and ongoing analysis of financial metrics not only helps in tracking the success of current initiatives but also aids in forecasting future financial conditions, enabling better preparation and strategic planning for long-term success.

OPERATIONAL METRICS

Operational metrics are essential for evaluating the efficiency and effectiveness of your processes and operations. These metrics provide valuable insights into how well your organization is functioning and where there may be opportunities for improvement. Key operational metrics may include measures such as process efficiency, cycle times, and defect rates, which are critical in assessing the overall performance of your operational activities.

Tracking operational metrics on a regular basis helps you identify specific areas where you can streamline processes, reduce costs, and improve quality. For instance, monitoring process efficiency can reveal bottlenecks that slow down production, while analyzing cycle times can help you understand how long it takes to complete a particular task or project. Additionally, keeping an eye on defect rates allows you to pinpoint quality issues that need to be addressed to maintain high standards.

Moreover, operational metrics provide a solid foundation for measuring the impact of your transformation efforts on your day-to-day operations. By continually monitoring these metrics, you can ensure that your organization is operating at peak efficiency and achieving its goals. This ongoing process of measurement and analysis enables you to make informed decisions, adapt to changing conditions, and drive continual improvement within your organization.

In summary, operational metrics are a crucial tool for any organization looking to optimize its performance. By providing a clear picture of how well your processes and operations are functioning, these metrics help you identify opportunities for improvement, track the success of your initiatives, and ensure that your organization is on the right path to achieving its strategic objectives.

CUSTOMER SATISFACTION METRICS

Customer satisfaction metrics are critical for understanding the impact of your transformation efforts on your customers. These metrics provide detailed insights into how well you are meeting customer needs and expectations and where there may be opportunities to improve the overall customer experience. Key customer satisfaction metrics may include customer satisfaction scores, net promoter scores, and customer retention rates, each of which offers a unique perspective on different aspects of customer satisfaction.

Tracking customer satisfaction metrics helps ensure that your transformation efforts are delivering tangible value to your customers and enhancing their experience with your organization. It also provides a solid foundation for identifying specific areas in which you can improve customer satisfaction and loyalty. For instance, if your customer satisfaction scores are lower than expected, you can delve deeper to understand the underlying reasons and address them effectively. Similarly, a low net promoter score might indicate that customers are not willing to recommend your services, signaling a need for immediate action to enhance their experience.

By regularly reviewing and analyzing your customer satisfaction metrics, you can ensure that your organization remains focused on delivering exceptional customer value. This regular review process allows you to make data-driven decisions that can lead to continual improvement in customer satisfaction and loyalty. Moreover, it helps in building a customer-centric culture within your organization, where every team member is aligned with the goal of providing the best possible customer experience. Ultimately, a strong focus on customer satisfaction metrics can drive long-term success and growth for your organization.

QUALITATIVE METRICS

In addition to quantitative metrics, qualitative metrics are also important for understanding the broader impact of your transformation efforts. These metrics provide insights into areas such as employee engagement, organizational culture, and stakeholder satisfaction. Key qualitative metrics may include employee feedback collected through interviews and focus groups, stakeholder surveys that gauge satisfaction and expectations, and comprehensive cultural assessments that evaluate the alignment of company values and behaviors.

Tracking qualitative metrics helps ensure that your transformation efforts are having a positive impact on your organization and its stakeholders. It also provides a basis for identifying areas in which you can enhance your organizational culture and build stronger relationships with your stakeholders. By regularly reviewing your qualitative metrics, you can ensure that your organization is fostering a positive and supportive environment. Furthermore, understanding these metrics allows leadership to make informed decisions about areas needing improvement and to celebrate areas of success. These metrics can also highlight trends over time, offering a longitudinal view of the organization's development and the effectiveness of its strategies.

REGULAR REVIEW AND ADAPTATION

Regular review and adaptation is critical for ensuring that your measurement system remains effective and relevant over time. This process involves continually reviewing your metrics and KPIs, evaluating their impact on your business objectives, and making necessary adjustments as needed. It also involves identifying new metrics and KPIs that reflect changing circumstances and evolving goals within your organization.

Regular review and adaptation not only helps ensure that your measurement system is providing meaningful insights but also drives continual improvement across various departments. This continual refinement process provides a solid basis for making informed decisions, optimizing your transformation efforts, and aligning your strategy with current market conditions. By continually reviewing and adapting your measurement system, you can ensure that your organization remains agile, proactive, and responsive to change, ultimately enhancing your competitive edge.

Moreover, regular review and adaptation creates a culture of accountability and transparency within your team. It encourages open communication about what is working and what could be improved, fostering a collaborative environment where everyone is focused on achieving common goals. In addition, this approach allows you to anticipate potential challenges and address them proactively, minimizing risks and maximizing opportunities for growth.

In summary, by committing to regular review and adaptation, you not only maintain the effectiveness of your measurement system but also empower your organization to thrive in an ever-changing business landscape.

THE ROLE OF FEEDBACK LOOPS

Feedback loops are an essential component of continual improvement. They provide a mechanism for gathering feedback, evaluating its impact, and making adjustments to optimize performance. Feedback loops can be internal, involving feedback from employees and stakeholders, or external, involving feedback from customers and partners.

Effective feedback loops involve more than just gathering feedback; they require a structured approach to evaluating and acting on feedback. This involves analyzing feedback, identifying trends and patterns, and making adjustments to improve performance. It also involves fostering a culture of openness and transparency where feedback is valued and acted upon.

CREATING A CULTURE OF CONTINUAL IMPROVEMENT

Creating a culture of continual improvement is critical for sustaining the momentum of your transformation efforts. This involves fostering an environment where employees are encouraged to seek out opportunities for improvement, take risks, and learn from their experiences. It also involves providing the tools and support needed to continually enhance performance and drive innovation.

A culture of continual improvement is built on a foundation of trust, collaboration, and accountability. It requires strong leadership, clear communication, and a commitment to learning and growth. By fostering a culture of continual improvement, you can ensure that your organization remains agile, innovative, and competitive.

Integrating continual improvement into your organizational culture requires a strategic and holistic approach. This involves embedding continual improvement into your values, practices, and processes. It also involves fostering a mindset of continual learning and growth so employees are encouraged to seek out new opportunities and embrace change.

All of this requires commitment—a consistent dedication to ongoing learning and development. This involves providing training and support, recognizing and rewarding innovation, and creating a supportive environment where employees feel valued and motivated. By integrating continual improvement into your organizational culture, you can ensure that your organization remains agile, responsive, and focused on achieving its goals.

EXAMPLES OF EFFECTIVE PERFORMANCE MEASUREMENT SYSTEMS

Throughout my career, I have often been recruited into companies to lead what is commonly referred to as a "turnaround" mission, but I prefer to call it a "growth-acceleration" mission. This journey has emphasized the critical importance of organizational alignment, the absence of which is often the primary obstacle to achieving growth acceleration. The evidence of this alignment challenge can be quantified through specific metrics, which then guide the identification and launch of initiatives to overcome these obstacles. As I consistently highlight in this book, "Everybody is in sales," and I'll illustrate this with a few examples.

In my roles at Wilson Golf and Brunswick, I was brought in to drive financial turnarounds. Drawing from my previous experiences at Gillette and Alberto Culver, we rigorously tracked a key metric known as the "fill rate"— the percentage of orders received, shipped, and accepted on time per the retailer's exact request. Retail giants such as Walmart, Target, Kroger, and Walgreens demanded a 98 percent fill rate, reflecting the precision needed to keep shelves stocked without excess inventory. For companies with complex product offerings, referred to as SKUs (stock keeping units), this metric was crucial. An order from a major retailer might include 25 SKU line items, each with specific quantities and delivery dates, leaving no room for error.

When I joined Wilson and Brunswick, I was particularly interested in this fill rate metric, as it often correlates with stalled revenue growth. Retailers operate on a "just-in-time" inventory system, aiming to minimize store-level inventory while avoiding empty shelves. The logic is straightforward: If a product is out of stock, consumers will likely purchase a competitor's product, resulting in lost sales. In such large-scale operations as Gillette's, where products are distributed to thousands of stores, failing to meet the 98 percent fill rate can significantly impact revenue growth. Achieving this rate is a clear organizational alignment challenge, involving accurate sales forecasting, manufacturing operations, inventory management, and a complex global supply chain.

Upon reviewing the fill rate audits at Wilson and Brunswick, the results were alarming. Unlike the best-in-class 98 percent fill rates at Gillette and Alberto Culver, these companies were struggling with fill rates in the range of 75 to 80 percent. This deficiency meant many consumers were leaving stores empty-handed or with competitors' products, costing us sales and hindering revenue growth.

To address these challenges, we needed to embrace the mantra that "everybody is in sales." This concept underscores that sales is not a singular function but a complex, multi-functional discipline that requires the coordination of various departments. At Wilson and Brunswick, we implemented regular multi-functional team meetings, involving representatives from all relevant areas. These meetings ranged from monthly to weekly, and even daily if necessary. We also held "multi-functional-team-selling" meetings with major customers, allowing all team leads to hear first-hand the expectations from retailers, including the critical 98 percent fill rate requirement.

By fostering this multi-functional alignment, we successfully elevated our fill rates to the industry-standard 98 percent. This improvement directly translated into accelerated sales and revenue growth, significantly contributing to the successful turnaround or "growth acceleration/desired future state" mission. The key to this success was a unified commitment to the idea that everyone in the organization plays a role in sales, working together as an aligned team to meet and exceed customer expectations.

CONCLUSION: THE PATH TO SUSTAINABLE SUCCESS

Measuring success and fostering a culture of continual improvement are critical for the long-term success of your transformation efforts.

By developing a comprehensive measurement system, regularly reviewing and adapting your metrics, and integrating continual improvement into your organizational culture, you can ensure that your organization remains agile, responsive, and focused on achieving its goals.

In the final chapter, we will reflect on the transformation journey, summarizing the key takeaways and discussing the long-term benefits of maintaining a desired future state. We will also explore the ongoing journey of organizational growth and transformation, providing a vision for the future and encouraging you to continue striving for excellence.

8

CONCLUSION AND
FUTURE DIRECTIONS

Interactive Video Chapter Summary

Or text **conclusion** to 855-426-7770

—⁜—

As you reach the end of your transformation journey, let's take a moment to step back and reflect on the path we've traveled together. It's been quite the ride, hasn't it? Over the past chapters, we've dug into the essential steps for driving a successful transformation: from assessing the current state to defining a clear vision, from developing a strategic roadmap to overcoming challenges and implementing change, each step has been crucial. Each step will shape your organization and guide you toward your desired future state.

Transformation is not a straight road—not by a long shot. It's a dynamic journey, filled with twists and turns, challenges and opportunities. It demands constant adaptation and resilience. As you reflect on this journey, let's appreciate the progress you've made. It helps you recognize the lessons you've learned. And it gets you ready for the ongoing process of growth and improvement.

Think about it: Every bump in the road and every obstacle you faced taught you something valuable. Every success, no matter how small, has brought you closer to your goals. It's been a rollercoaster, but it's also been incredibly rewarding.

So what's next? Well, transformation doesn't stop here. It's an ongoing journey. You're always learning, always growing. And that's exciting, because with every step you take, you're not just moving forward—you're evolving. You're becoming better.

In the end, it's about the journey as much as the destination. It's about pushing boundaries and daring to dream big. It's about not settling for the status quo. And it's about believing in the vision you've set for yourself and your organization.

So keep going. Keep pushing. The journey doesn't end here. In fact, it's just beginning.

KEY TAKEAWAYS FROM THE TRANSFORMATION JOURNEY

Looking back on your journey, several key takeaways stand out. These insights have been instrumental in driving your transformation and will continue to guide you as you move forward:

1. **The Importance of Vision:** A clear and compelling vision is the foundation of any successful transformation. It provides direction, inspires action, and aligns your organization toward a common goal. Your vision is your guiding star, helping you navigate the challenges and stay focused on your long-term objectives.

2. **The Power of Assessment:** Understanding where you are before you embark on the transformation journey is crucial. Your comprehensive assessment of your organization's current state provides a clear baseline, identifies key areas for improvement, and informs your strategic planning.

3. **The Value of Strategic Planning:** A well-thought-out strategic plan is essential for bridging the gap between the current state and the desired future state. Your strategic plan provides a roadmap for action, guiding your efforts and

ensuring that you stay on track toward your goals.

4. **The Role of Leadership:** Effective leadership is critical in driving transformation. As a leader, you play a key role in setting the vision, fostering a culture of change, and guiding your team through the challenges of the journey. Your leadership is instrumental in maintaining momentum and achieving your goals.

5. **The Necessity of Change Management:** Managing change effectively is crucial for the success of any transformation. Your change management strategies will help you navigate resistance, build support, and ensure that your team is prepared for and engaged in the transformation process.

6. **The Importance of Continual Improvement:** Transformation is an ongoing journey, not a one-time event. Your commitment to continual improvement will help you adapt to changing circumstances, seize new opportunities, and ensure that your organization remains agile and competitive.

LONG-TERM BENEFITS OF MAINTAINING A DESIRED FUTURE STATE

Achieving a desired future state is a significant milestone, but it is not the end of the journey. It's a new beginning that brings numerous long-term benefits for your organization. By maintaining your focus on the desired future state, you can continue to drive growth, innovation, and success. Some of the key long-term benefits include:

1. **Sustained Competitive Advantage:** By continually adapting and improving, you can maintain a competitive edge in the market, responding to changes and seizing new opportunities as they arise.

2. **Enhanced Organizational Agility:** A commitment to continual improvement helps build organizational agility, enabling you to respond quickly to changes in the market and adapt to new challenges and opportunities.

3. **Improved Operational Efficiency:** Ongoing efforts to streamline processes and improve operations help ensure

that you remain efficient and effective, reducing costs and increasing productivity.

4. **Increased Employee Engagement:** A focus on continual improvement fosters a positive organizational culture where employees feel valued, motivated, and engaged in their work. This leads to higher levels of job satisfaction and retention.

5. **Greater Customer Satisfaction:** By continually improving your products and services, you can better meet the needs and expectations of your customers, enhancing their satisfaction and loyalty.

A VISION FOR THE ONGOING JOURNEY

The journey of transformation is never truly over. It's an ongoing process that requires constant vigilance, adaptation, and a commitment to excellence. As you look to the future, it's important to maintain a vision for ongoing growth and transformation. This vision should be dynamic, evolving as your organization and the market change and providing a clear direction for future efforts.

Your vision for the future should be bold and ambitious, reflecting your commitment to innovation and excellence. It should inspire your team to continue striving for greatness, and it should guide you as you navigate the challenges and opportunities that lie ahead. By maintaining a clear vision for the future, you can ensure that your organization remains focused, motivated, and ready to achieve its goals.

Throughout this journey, we have been inspired by the achievements of others and the wisdom of those who have come before us. These examples remind us of the power of perseverance, the importance of vision, and the potential for greatness that lies within each of us.

A quote that has resonated with me throughout my career is from Henry Ford: "Coming together is a beginning; keeping together is progress; working together is success." This quote encapsulates the essence of our transformation journey—the importance of unity, collaboration, and shared purpose in achieving our goals.

As we conclude this book, I encourage you to take actionable steps toward your own transformation journey. Reflect on where you are today, define your vision for the future, and develop a strategic plan to guide your efforts. Embrace change, foster a culture of continual improvement, and commit to ongoing growth and excellence.

Remember, transformation is not just about achieving a desired future state; it's about continually striving for improvement and pushing the boundaries of what is possible. By taking these steps, you can ensure that your organization remains agile, competitive, and ready to seize the opportunities of the future.

This is not the end, but rather the beginning of a new chapter. The principles and strategies we've discussed will continue to guide you as you navigate the challenges and opportunities of the future. Transformation is an ongoing journey that requires continual effort, adaptation, and a commitment to excellence.

By maintaining a clear vision, fostering a culture of continual improvement, and embracing change, you can ensure that your organization remains on the path to success. The journey of transformation is never truly over, but with the right mindset and approach, you can achieve lasting success and create a brighter future for your organization.

As you move forward, I encourage you to keep these principles in mind, remain open to new ideas and opportunities, and continue striving for greatness. The journey of transformation is challenging, but the rewards are well worth the effort. I wish you the best of luck on your journey, and I look forward to seeing the incredible things you will achieve.

EPILOGUE

—⟋⟍—

INTELLISMART—MOBILE-VIDEO INTERACTIVE CHAPTER SUMMARIES

Throughout this book, you may have noticed the inclusion of "Intellismart-Video-Interactive-Book-Pages." These pages leverage proprietary technology from my Web3.0 MarComTech company, Didgebridge, to integrate QR codes with SMS text, delivering mobile-video summaries of each chapter.

This Intellismart technology is designed to enhance your reading experience by combining the written word with video, sound, and motion. With your consent, it also offers the opportunity to "opt-in" and establish a personalized "SMS-loyalty-channel" with the author and/or publisher. My background in psychology, combined with my experience at Kodak, has given me a deep appreciation for the human brain's capacity as an audio-visual processor. The mission of Desired Future

State's Intellismart is to deepen your engagement by merging text with dynamic, multimedia content.

If you're interested in staying connected, you can create a private Web3.0 loyalty channel that allows us to keep in touch and update you on future books and projects. Our Web3.0 ComTek is designed to protect your privacy, preventing Web2.0 data mining of our loyalty channels. Unlike other Web2.0 technologies, we never share or sell your private, consensual Intellismart loyalty data.

DESIRED FUTURE STATE— ANNUAL PERFORMANCE PLANS FOR EACH EMPLOYEE

During my career, I've overseen organizations with thousands of employees, and I began to use the concept of Desired Future State as the foundation for each employee's personalized annual performance plan. This plan is collaboratively developed by the employees and their immediate supervisors and is reviewed monthly.

As a C-suite leader, I witnessed the GROWTH-acceleration benefits of this collaborative approach. It became clear that the success of each employee's Desired Future State plan was directly linked to the overall success of the organization. In fact, it became a predictive indicator of success—not just for individual business units, but also for the entire organization. When individual goals are met or missed, these outcomes can be aggregated to provide a clear, easily monitored prediction of the organization's end-of-year performance.

For C-suite leaders interested in deeper insights, we offer a customized Intellismart-Web3.0 mobile app. This app allows managers, from the CEO on down, to gain predictive insight into the progress of each business unit's Desired Future State annual plan, tracking both unit and individual employee progress.

In closing, I want to thank you for taking the time to read *Desired Future State*. I hope this systematic approach to change management and GROWTH acceleration has been beneficial for your organization and possibly even for you personally. If you're interested, I'd be delighted to invite you into my PRIVATE Intellismart loyalty network, where I can keep you updated on future book projects and related insights. If you're a C-suite leader and would like to learn more about our Desired Future State Web3.0 mobile app for your organization, I'm happy to discuss that as well. I appreciate your interest and wish you great success in achieving your personal and organizational Desired Future State.

www.ingramcontent.com/pod-product-compliance
Lightning Source LLC
Chambersburg PA
CBHW021930190326
41519CB00009B/970